The Sauntering Eye
Kansas Meditations

Elizabeth Schultz

FUTURECYCLE PRESS
www.futurecycle.org

Published by FutureCycle Press
Hayesville, North Carolina, USA

ISBN 978-1-938853-48-7

Contents

3.

Unusual Weather

4.

The Death of Bivalves

1.

*Kansas Places: Wetlands, Prairies,
Fields, Woods, River*

The Medicine Wheel

The compass in the grass
stretches out across an acre,
designates the four directions,
bear claws to the west,
mountains north and south,
thunderbird to the east,
spreading wings among trees.

A stone altar marks each way.
In the center, a fire circle
filled with ash brings it all
together. At the markers,
amulets—agates, batteries,
coins, barrettes, an earring,
a plastic heart—frayed
by weather, charm the seasons.
Waving from trees, colored
flags, faded yearnings.

Oceanic Journey

On a May morning in Kansas
we set out from harbor,
over the bottom of this old sea,
moss-green as a tortoise's back,
mists erasing the horizon,
waves washing the sky,
and buzzards swimming
and sighing above us.

Ishmaelian Me

Clouds billowing and boiling,
exposing sky a larkspur blue,
highway lines unfurling
across a swelling landscape,
passing rocky promontories,
rough-and-tumble grasses,
undulating, Jarrett blending
cadences on the blue tooth.
I drive, I drift, the car a gently
rolling ship. I grasp the wheel
at precisely nine and three
and rock on toward that elusive
and deep, blue, bottomless soul.

Prairie Immersion: After 9/11

The prairie swept me away, wave
upon wave of green, rising and falling
in mist. I paused, dissolved as spindrift
on a limestone crest, to let the prairie
float me up onto a distant edge, then dash
me back to this hard point, where sky
and land conspired to pin me under
a glare of silence in the turning, aching
world, permitting me at last to descend,
to go out through a trough of flowers.

Out of Sight

On a fast track, hit and run
across the plains, or even
just passing through, you may
miss the body of the supine land,
the beast's shaggy pelt, hirsute
with unshaven grasses, pulsating,
flexing, not to mention the grasses'
tousled masses of roots, their dark
viscera, stretching to the ends
of the earth, beyond boundaries,
out of sight.

A Short History of Burning Kansas

Lightning touched the grass.
It flared and raced.

Red Buffalo, the Cheyenne called it,
watching the charge across the plains.
Myriad hooves sparked flames
against the flinty soil, and dust
rose up in searing clouds of smoke.
Galloping beside it, ahead of it,
maneuvering their horses through
fleeing antelope, rabbits, coyotes,
every year they anticipated flight.

Quantrill roared into town.
His raiders struck their tinderboxes,
burned the hotel, shops, houses.
They fired their rifles, killed
the preacher man and 142 more.
They ignited a war.

News Item: 4:00 a.m., she flicked on
the cafe's hot-water heater
and was dropping doughnuts
into boiling oil when the asphalt
in the alley exploded. The apartment
next door churned into a blazing
tornado. Fire climbed the sky,
unrolled tongues of flame across the street.
Scorched, she escaped from hell to tell.
Two sleeping students were asphyxiated,
and I moved away from burning buildings.

Fire is choreography,
is necklaces strung out
glittering across fields
in controlled burns.

Photographed, flames
appear to liquefy flowers
and lick the moon.

Forest fires ravaging Oregon,
a haze of ash wafts over Kansas.
The charred prairie turns green again.

Spring Burning

Anticipating
sumptuous vistas,
we went to the prairie
to find it burned
black and smoldering,
the horizon glowering
saffron with ash,
blistered with embers.
The scent of scorched
grass and charred cities
thrashed us. Our mouths
filled with cinders
from distant lands.

Spring Equinox

The earth tilted.
The sun trembled on the horizon,
then toppled us into darkness.
We responded with fire, sending
sparks to the stars. We huddled,
recalling the morning: marching,
the coffins' weight on our shoulders,
the year of burning, of singed dreams.
We walked back to the cars, guided
by the frogs' exuberance.

The Sauntering Eye

I have the habit of attention to such excess
that my senses get no rest, but suffer from
a constant strain.... What I need is not
to look at all, but a true sauntering of the eye.

—Henry David Thoreau

A spring day
in the wetlands
is sensational.

Colors sizzle.
Sound, scent,
and breeze twitch.

Insect, bird,
and reptile tingle.
Grasses gyrate.

Water riffles, and
you are blitzed
with razzle-dazzle.

Panting, you rise
and glide with
the great white egret.

Enthralled, you listen
to chats and warblers
rhapsodize.

Loitering, you notice
that light strokes
each stalk of grass.

Spring Jazz

Spring swings
in the wetlands:
scintillating jazz,
dawn-to-dusk
exuberance of
improvisations
over frog croak,
blackbird creak,
grackle cackle,
dried aster crackle,
air hums,
woodpecker drums,
rabbit frisks,
skink shimmies,
trill of warbler solo,
riff of drifting hawk,
behind it all,
water rippling,
earth rumbling
as snakes slither,
grasses sigh,
possums snuffle,
beavers splash,
turtles plop,
geese whoop,
while during
this simultaneity,
this multiplicity,
the algae silently
spreads.

Margins

The highway makes a clean cut
through the wetlands. It straightens
things out, speeding the passage
of trucks and machines, but leaves
unruly margins where the spiel
of tires mingles with the throttle
of insects, the shriek of hawks,
and you find your way by pausing.
Then, there's time to sniff out
the palpitating lives of voles.

Loss of Light

At twilight, there's a ruckus
in the wetlands: response
to the loss of light. Geese,
anxious, rise perturbed into
the air. Sparrows, clicking,
chattering, settle in among
brambles. Grasses are restless.

It happens soundlessly.
No switch is flipped.
The light simply seeps away
over the rise. Its last traces,
ochre and rose, dissolve as
the dark door closes silently,
leaving an illuminated crack
from the other room.
Stars don't click on, and
the moon, as always, is calm
as an egg, knowing light is
still everywhere.

Last Day of Summer

On this last day of summer,
I come with friends to watch
the sun set over the wetlands.
Its great blaze burns the clouds.
They turn ashen but still glow
with coals, and the blackbirds
sweep like cinders overhead.

Apocalypse is on my mind
and the sickness of my friend.
Still these wetlands are full
of pulsations, of cricket and frog
susurrations, the impertinence
of geese honk and duck holler.
The sky inhales light.

Shade thickens, extracting color
from thistles and sunflowers.
Ripeness recedes, and against
the last light, grasses darken
in intricate designs. The moon,
a slender handle in the door of
night, opens to a cascade of stars.

Thanksgiving Day

The sky, streaked grey,
bars the sun. The canals
are hard-packed, cracked
into paving stones. Edges,
rimmed with slime, are
stamped with the hooves
of deer seeking water.
Spent pods and berries
spangle the brush tangles.

Sparrows dash in and out
of the bushes. Their nests,
still architecturally sound,
hang like abandoned fruit.
Furred by thistle and cattail
seeds, desiccated sunflower
stalks shine, and wild rose
vines glow like arteries. Their
thorns gleam. Grasses bend
and sway, and the landscape
of drought continues to rustle.

November Meditations

1.

November is Puritan grey,
a penultimate month, somber
and chilling, inserted between
Halloween phantasmagoria
and Christmas extravagances.
Fall's flaming turns ashen.
Leaves disintegrate in the gutter.
In November, some ship out to sea.

2.

The wetlands are a near port.
Edged by thicket and grey woods,
they are closer than oceans.
I plunge in.

Summer's screens of greenery
are down, but trees are snared
by shrubs, twined in vines.
I leave gloom snagged on thorns.

In this leafless tangle, a throng
surrounds me—rose hips, bittersweet,
coral bush, honeysuckle berries.
Everywhere red eyes stare.

3.

Space opens. Water shines.
In the darkest time, thickets
give way to flashing sedges
and flowing grasses. Light
sweeps them, kindling colors.
The November wetlands
are committed to action.

The grasses toss their heads
to the winds, scattering seeds
with serious abandon.

Bedraggled cattails flick
their fluff about. Milkweed
pods erupt with spinning silk.
Even the dour and stiffened
wetland flowers—aster,
sunflower, bundle weed—
hold up small chalices of seeds
to sprinkle over time.

So skies seethe with a shimmer
of seeds ejaculating through
the air, lighting on earth,
wiggling down into darkness
where, wily and wild, they
prepare for a takeover in March.

4.

Imprinted trails provide
a guestbook of wetland visitors.
Sneakers and dogs' paws
are stamped over the signatures
of the wetlands' regular inhabitants,
those with proprietary interest.

Read the traffic signs: a packet
of scat opened to show
indigestible lizard skin, claws,
and ivory fangs; palm prints
of raccoons; an articulated
spinal section, probably coyote;
and then, a black snake, sinuous
in its death scroll, the hawk's
puncture wounds stapled into
its back, a butter-yellow belly
exposed, while in the shrubs
a living twin uncoils. Leaving
no track, in slithering pen, it
writes indelibly across memory.

5.

Invisible in these cold
waters, beavers breathe.
Obscured among reeds,
they pause. They doze.
They ruminate and wait.

Teased by signs—
crisply cut saplings,
a slippery trail,
mud-slathered banks—
I know they're here.

I catch the crack
of water smacked and
watch a wake dissolving.
The pond stills, wiped
clean of sound and motion.

My yearning for beavers
is unrequited. As beavers
keep their splashy affairs
so private, the audience
is irrelevant.

6.

Some dismiss the little birds
in favor of great raptors,
the herons, and the geese.

The little birds—all
variations of sparrow—
signify no heroic drama.

They spend their days
twittering in the grasses.
Skittish, they do not pose.
They flicker in and out of
light and cast no shadows.

Overhead, snow geese,
winding and unwinding,
roll up the sky in folds.

And a red-tail, dropping,
suddenly splits that seamless
fabric. But the insignificant

little birds, tacking the sky
to its horizon, keep us
grounded and social.

7.

In Kansas, hedge apples lie
under trees—gigantic marbles.
Kids roll them down steep
streets, watching them jump
the curb at the bottom or
just smash into pulp, each one
an alien green brain, each one
oozing white milk.

In Michigan and Massachusetts,
the smooth Granny Smith was
the only green apple, making
the lumpy hedge apple seem
a Disney creation. Settlers,
I learned later, brought them
inside to repel cockroaches.

In Kansas, when the curtain
of leaves drops, hedge apples
are revealed, ornamenting the trees
as chartreuse orbs. As if part of
an elitist designer's scheme,
they hang, here and there, decking
November's puritanical woods
with mystic phosphorescence.

Deep Freeze: New Year's Day, 2009

Last night the blue moon
hung frozen in space,
and now on this first day
of the year, the sun can't
burn through the evening's
grey shoals of clouds.

The wetlands where I walk
have drifted into whiteness.
Canals and marshes are set
in ice, and snow encrusted,
the grasses bow down. Geese
are leaving the chilled land,
undulating above me.

A harrier, hovering intent over
the grasses at mid-range, freezes
into place, and sparrows, skittish
in the brush, flee. The snow shows
one small bird's final fluttering,
preserved fan-like, pressed
into the snow with a red streak.

I read erratic mice tracks, circling
and intersecting with the scrolling
calligraphy of a possum's tail:
in a search against starvation,
scarcely casual jottings. Dark dirt
flung up onto whiteness reveals
desperate digging for security.

The cold numbs my fingertips,
and I've had enough of plotting
my course across the snow field.
Hunkering deeper into my down
coat, I follow my tracks back,
grateful my comfort is not yet below
the snow line in the hard, dark earth.

How to Read a Winter Field

Summer's illuminated manuscript is gone.
Nothing green or luxuriant remains.
The field of snow is a severe parchment.

A few autumn grasses penetrate the crust.
Collaborating with the wind, thin stalks
and seed heads scratch back and forth.

This field of snow reveals some basics.
Spring's eruption of green never shows
so much as this plain whiteness where

rabbits, mice, coyotes inscribe frenzied
survival. Throughout the winter, they track
the field with their skittish narratives.

Their deaths, out in the open, blot it red
while beneath the snow, voles and weasels knot
into warmth, where no fundamentalist tract

in white and black spells out their dreams.

Redbuds

Before there is a sign of green,
hard red beads appear knotted
together on dark branches, drops
of blood squeezed from winter.

Sap and sun work, then, to swell
the buds, to open them petal by petal,
staining the branches magenta.

Later, redbuds expand into rose-
tinted clouds, diffused through woods,
along the edge of meadows.

The blossoms fuse with cherry,
peach, and plum, flesh out Kansas
hills and fields with pulsating pink

until they are exhausted, bleeding
each year in incarnadine circles
beneath their trunks, making way
again for the trees' heart-shaped leaves.

Diversity

In nature, it seems easy:
the sycamore's white arms
embrace the hackberry's
dark trunk, and the woods
rejoice as they grow
together.

The Oak in My Front Yard

On a windless summer day,
I wonder how the limbs of the pin oak
in my front yard can branch straight
out from its great trunk, defying gravity,
sprawling into space, and so comfortable
in the stretch, only its leaves tremble.

When the wind is up and a storm
is on, the oak remains a steady
perpendicular though the branches
swoop and holler and all the leaves
shimmy. The oak dances in place,
celebrates swishing sun and shade
and the rain shining down to its roots.

Skeletal in winter, its crotches
warm nests of squirrels, and
a cardinal appears, a beating heart,
among the tangle of its dark limbs.
The sap flow slows, pulling sugar
from permafrost, reaching
to the tips of twigs, crackling.

The oak spreads through wires,
and chainsaws cut a gap in its girth.
Then the sapling in the center of
the oak's rings remembers swelling
grasslands before this yard, this house.
It litters the lawn with acorns, attending
to the future.

Oak Trees in December

Maple, elm, and ash, long since,
have dropped their loads onto
lawns and into loam and eaves.

But in the woods and in our yards,
oak trees still hold their leaves,
like bag ladies clutching debris,
excess brown paper bags, tattered
remnants of an earlier green glory.
Despite sneering winds, the oak trees
hold their own, waiting for the right
season to let down their leaves and hair.

Dornwood

The wild grapevine
swings among the trees,
twisting and twining,
weaving hackberry
to oak, oak to hickory.
Its ropes, darkened
and knotted, give
free passage to light
and birds, but we are
held back, nightmares
snagged in the dream
catcher's convolutions.

The Unseen Life

Beneath the thick woods,
the littered ground, mat
and mess of leaves, trees
toppled, rotting, sinking,
mildewing into amalgam
of matter, moist, dense,
permeated with swelling,
sweating microorganisms,
myriad and mutating,
fermenting, the mycelia
of fungi, frail and ghostly,
yeasty, spreading out into
mesh and web, creeping
beneath the thick woods,
the rhizomorphs invisible
unless you choose to look
for the little lower layer,
beyond the fruiting body,
the flashy flesh, unless
you leave no log unturned.

The Calm Place

The calm place isn't far away.
You cut across the freeway,
take two-lane roads outside the city,
drive across a field, enter woods.
There is a path among the trees—
hackberry, bur oak, walnut,
and the glistening, skeletal sycamores.
Shuffling through leaves, you are
your own noise. High overhead,
bare limbs swivel against the sky,
while down below, a nameless
creek wears a sedate course through
limestone layers. It pools in stillness,
pressing myriad leaves together in
an underwater book, its deckle edges
unturned, unread. There is a prayer
in this place if you'll remember
to ask directions.

Watching the Kansas River

Who looks upon a river
in a meditative hour
and is not reminded
of the flux of all things?*

—Ralph Waldo Emerson

*My soul has grown
deep like the rivers.*

—Langston Hughes

1.

Tumescent in the spring,
the brown river surges.
It is swollen with desire.

It is sleek and slick,
its sheen spreading
as the heat rises.
Spume laps its edges.
The river foams.

It charges, lunging,
leaping in its channel.
It discovers its depth.

The river is self-generating.

2.

turgid,
turbulent,
tumultuous
tumbling,
rumbling,
stumbling,
mumbling,

grumbling,
rambling,
roiling,
rocking,
rolling,
rushing,
roaring,
pell-melling,
cascading,
catapulting,
churning,
turning,
twining,
winding,
swelling,
gathering
leaves, twigs, logs,
dogs, cars, cows,
carcasses unto itself,
continuous,
continuing,
ongoing,
onward.

3.

On the stillest days,
when the river wears
satin, it is never still.

On the stillest days,
when its tangled banks
are seen mirrored

in the current, it rustles
and groans, seethes, sighs
in conversation with itself.

With the ruffling wind,
the reflections ripple
and morph into mosaics.

4.

Five fishermen are stationed
on rocks along the river.
They are as patient as sages
in Chinese ink paintings.
One sits in a crumpled plastic
chair. Their lines curve out from
their rods, vanish into the river.

Caught in an eddy mid-river,
two tree trunks gyrate slowly
like the hands of a clock.
Following a metronome
of their own, swallows swoop
in and out beneath the bridge.
A heron stands by, stalk still.

There is no sign of fish.
The river reveals nothing:
only its currents' quick curl.
Like centuries of the faithful,
the fishermen believe in what
they cannot see, anticipating
the miraculous jolt.

Legends ride the river—
catfish monstrous enough
to swallow rifles, stagecoaches,
immense enough to feed three
neighborhoods, men wily
enough to wrestle gar eye-
to-eye with the river rising.

The line straightens. The rod bends.
The fisherman braces his feet.
Any minute now, an expulsion
of carp, bullhead, drum fish,
crappy, sturgeon. The bait is
taken and landed with its poisonous
package of PCBs and mercury.

The fishermen return tomorrow
to the gut-smeared rocks along the river.
They fish until the swallows vanish.
They fish although they do not see.
They throw back some small fry.
They scale some cat for super.
The fishermen return tomorrow.

5.

It moves alongside us.
It passes beneath us.
It swishes around us.

It shapes our boundaries.
It bears our history.
It permeates our dreams.

We use it. We disturb it.
We name it. We claim it.
We touch it. It touches us.

6.

Glacial melt,
draining south,
meandering
over floodplains,
through clay,
sand, gravel, loess,
around boulders,
named by and for
the Kanza people,
who drank it
and bathed in it,
first mapped
by a Frenchman
in 1718, 170 miles
free-flowing from
the confluence
of the Republican
and the Smoky Hill

to the Missouri,
four miles wide
at Wamego, easy
going for canoes
and pirogues,
stymieing steamboats
with its mud,
dug up by dredges
reaping its sand,
after excessive rain,
cresting its banks
drowning beasts
and men for centuries,
a wilderness river,
polluted and damaged,
called the Kaw
by those who still
watch it.

7.

A turtle shell hung
on my apartment wall,
a decoration as large
as a shield. It was worn
and scored, but the sea
had polished it to a gleam.

A turtle shell hung
on my apartment wall
commemorating those
who live for 10,000 years,
who shaped the continent,
who support the globe.

A turtle shell hung
on my apartment wall,
until the night we tipped
it into the river, sending
it swirling back to the sea.

8.

In a canoe on the river
we can go with the flow
or maneuver against its grain.
Either way, the river moves us.

Along the bank, we drift
with orioles sewing gaudy
orange into a green canopy
of cottonwoods and willows.

Paddling the central channel,
we ride a progressive current
around bends, past sand bars,
into rapids, spellbound by speed.

Along the bank, we drift
among beavers who wink
and vanish, leaving us to follow
in a great blue heron's wake.

Paddling the central channel,
we swerve around a tree, roots
exposed and straining the river
of its plastic bags and condoms.

Along the bank, we drift
among cottonwood seeds spun
out on currents of air, light-filled
and leisurely in their wandering.

9.

On a sandbar
a heron is laid
out with care.
A dream catcher,
its design is
pressed into sand.

Its wings stretch
in skeletal symmetry.
Feathers crochet
its light bones.
Its feet curl into
dark amulets,
and its beak is
a polished blade.
Scarabs bead
its intricate fretwork.
Relentlessly,
remorselessly,
the shining insects
devour the design,
releasing the bird
into a river of light.

10.

One winter the eagles return.
Up and down the frozen river,
they stake themselves out in
the cottonwoods' dark branches.
Their gaze is imperial,
their shadows are iron on the ice,
their beaks refined devices.
Glinting in the sun, their white
helmets flash like steel.

11.

The river freezes.
Its urgency is sedated.
Its deep brown pales.
Ghost-like,
it lies on the land,
the translucent skin
of its serpentine self.
The river thaws.
It puddles the sky.
Its scales shine.

Between stripes
of white, it uncoils
ribbons of sunset.
Unseen under ice,
the river stirs.

12.

At night the river is
opaque. It rolls thick
as black oil and
takes all prisoners.

It consumes the night,
the shadows of trees.
It swallows the glint of
campfires and animal eyes.

On a midnight dare,
a man sets out swimming
across the river, steady
and swift, self-assured.

He did not foresee
a deadhead collision
or his body, snagged,
twisting and turning.

A girl, craving darkness,
leaps from the bridge.
She is buried in water,
rushing and rinsing.

A naked boy stands on
the shore, his piss aspiring
toward the river. He listens
for the fusion of streams.

13.

In August,
in a season of drought,
consider the river,
pursuing its course
through a sandbar maze,
reconfiguring the land,
feeling its way forward,
finger by fluid finger.

Sucking and sighing,
it sieves through sand,
which rearranges
itself, accommodating
the carcasses of cars
and cows, absorbing
invisible chemicals
and unknown protozoa.
As clouds in a streaming
sky, islands of sand
emerge in the flowing
river, their shifty shores
straining to release
its water from putrefaction.

So dreams filter
the drifting night
of uncertainty's detritus,
buoying me, over and over,
restoring me to morning.

14.

Once we waded in the river.
Once we swam in the river.
Once we danced, sitting down,
while the river circled
and gurgled around us.

2.

Kansas: Hot and Cold

Heat Sequence: In and Out of Dreams

1.

Midsummer, midday,
the heat's agenda
demands full attention.
Sweat outlines all actions.
I yearn to slide fish-like
between sheets, slippery cool,
drowning in memories
of forest-rimmed lakes.

Inside, I shrink
among echoes of splashing.
Gestures are diminished,
pressed close against
bodies which once floated
in an expansive life.
Deprived of adjectives,
I am reduced to hand-me-down
thoughts, a scratched-out
existence in second-hand air.
Shades, drawn, keep me
in darkness, separated
from the white parchment
outside.

The AC is belly-up,
a dead horse corrosive
in the basement.
Its sixty years spewing
leisured ease in cyborg
service are over, and
I am left, tongue-swollen,
sweat-slathered, as flat
as cats and squirrels
stretched out, each hair
grasping the random breeze.

During these bright afternoons,
I hallucinate pioneers who cut
the roads and sod, who later,
in celluloid collars and nipped
waists, took their lemonade
on wraparound porches,
but I soon sink back into
my cicada self, suppressed
to chirring yearning for dark
hours of jazz.

2.

The air travels
the shoreless sky.
Gathering spin above
the shining Sahara,
it churns to fire,
swirling across seas
lingering and jostling
with coastal leaves.
Reaching the prairies,
it presses the grasses,
scorching them with
swathes of whiteness.
An invisible tyrant,
it fastens on whatever
is there, clutching,
shape-shifting.

Spiked, horned, and
thorned, the desert plants
and animals are prepared.
Succulents package moisture.
But no Eden ever anticipates
how the gates of heat fling open
in the sky, how the sun scorches
through the trees, dissolving
all distinctions in the garden.

Sounds diminish
beneath the cicadas' shrill.
Fountains shower powder.
Birds bathe in dust.
Beetles glitter.
With fangs gone brittle,
ferocity turns to lassitude,
and in the feverish shade,
the lion wilts with the lamb.

800 miles away,
Montana burns.
Fire climbs mountains,
reels across streams,
transforming clouds
to an asphalt of smoke.
In Kansas, it rains ash,
and the air sears
lungs and thighs.
There's little to see:
a mouse in the toilet,
the occasional bird,
head blazing featherless,
leaves by the curb
rattling like fall.

When the air fills
with fiery quivers
and razors burn
in the dry ground,
whimpering is over.
Dreaming oases,
birds, mice, fish
journey toward
gutters and eaves,
into house cats' claws.

Relinquishing
feathers and fur,
their scales singed,
they cross flaming
margins in a lust
for moist life.

Hummingbirds ride
out the sirocco
on the backs of ducks.
En route they pause—
shimmering hesitations,
sipping the last
of gladiolus nectar—
before all flowers
collapse into husks.
Monarchs cease
winging it and catch
the drafts, drifting
partway down to Mexico.
Other insects, too close
to atmospheric fires,
are pulverized orange
and red at sunset.
Dust settles, and slowly
the night-blooming cereus
glides, gondola-like,
glowing alabaster,
into the heaving dark.

In the dark,
the large animals
come out, rising up
on their haunches,
snorting, pawing the air.
As the shadows cool,
their hides crackle.
Their hairs twirl.
They levitate on stench.

3.

Together we watched
the sky, day after day,
a taut canvas
of blistering blue.
Together we watered
the earth, day after day,
a thirsting blotter.
On the day we saw
the pear tree shrivel,
the eggplants blacken,
the long white bones
of the land emerge,
we cursed our fate,
we capitulated to dust
and came inside for shade.

He plays the guitar,
day after day, dabbling
in exotic languages.
I dawdle over sherbet,
weeping for the loss
of lilies and apricots.

In obsession's heat, a vision
eases like a brief breeze
across the scalding brow:
in another land, two people
journey together in a canoe
through mist toward an island.
It is early morning.
Soundlessly, their shoulders
rise and fall. Their paddles
synchronized, they glide
forward into silver stillness.
A deer swims alongside them,
antlers, glistening in dew,
held high like a chandelier.
The island awaits somewhere.

In the days of burning air,
I dream of opening a window
to see geese boomeranging
overhead, to hear them
honking directly in my ear,
reminding me of other
patterns for survival.

Compelled by fox spirit,
three times Basho brought
his poems to the fox
to sniff out words,
precise, elusive, exquisite.
I've heard rumor of a fox
by our river, rustling
among late summer cattails,
hardly concerned with poems.
Its brush and ears,
tapered and alert, appear
in my dreams, assurance
that warblers and owls
have escaped the inferno.

4.

Fire continues with sumac,
its flamey leaves, leaping
one after the other uphill,
igniting the ivy into fiery
cords to throttle the hackberry
until the whole hillside burns:
a seasonal occurrence,
this glorious quickening,
and each time I wonder
how to prevent such kindling
from dwindling into embers.

Tension quickens as we wait:
cicadas and crickets still,
a few drops of rain, scattered

applause before the curtain
of heat rises and the orchestra
announces, with crescendos,
a cosmic performance. Glare
cracks the sky helter-skelter,
and rain's silver axes slash
at the iron earth. Such drama
brings down the house, and
we drown in desires fulfilled.

Windows are opened.
I hear crickets wheeze,
persimmons pinging
off the roof, bees slurping
syrup in the pears,
the geese's tribal honk,
gyrations in the grass:
      life turning
      and returning
      deep down,
      deep inland.

The ash tree holds out its golden bough.
The sky flares up. Saved by seasonal
rhythm, we are translated into ripeness.

Pacing the field
for the last time,
circling closer
toward the center,
the fox lassoes summer
in tight around him,
pulling nose into tail.
Beneath frost, the fox
dreams of cavorting
through grape arbors
and persimmon groves,
of frisking with hares,
of pursuing lushness
and glowing orbs.

Clamorous

In the heat, a clamorous life persists.
Sprinklers swirl. The air rasps.
There is riot in the grass. Beneath
the trees, children propel themselves
sky-high in swings and teeter-totters,
leaning back, kicking their heels.
A Chinese family tries Frisbee, flinging
the discus toward the setting sun's
red saucer. Swinging a golf club
at an invisible wasp, a man protests,
"It's mad. I don't know at what."

Air Conditioning

I keep the AC on, steady
drone of cool across my neck,
frosting my ears and elbows.
Its buzz erases outside traffic.

Insulated from rasping heat,
I lean into my computer, chunk
of white ice. Chlorofluorocarbons
chill my floor and feet.

I remember movie houses,
promoting cold interiors,
banners of parading penguins,
polar bears sliding on glaciers.

I hear a Japanese wind chime
tingling. Shadows slip
through reed shades, filter
the afternoon's hot weight.

I wait until fireflies appear.
When their heat lights the grass,
I will open my windows to air,
conditionally.

August Evening

A draft probes the furnace blast
though cicadas persist, their
shrill incessant and insistent.
Secure in the car's shadow,
a cat lounges under an SUV.
A motorcycle screeches to stop
for a rabbit darting into the street.

Twelve-year-old Luca insists
reality exists in a ten-mile radius
around him. "Why does he believe
such a thing?" his mother asks.
"I am vainglorious!" he proclaims,
tossing himself back on the grass,
considering the far-out appeal
of a coral reef seething with color.

A man crouched into his mobile
chair turns at a busy corner and
churns down the quiet street.
A woman texts in a rattan chair
on her front porch. In the western
sky, clouds froth and foam, emerging
as continents, revealing bays, fjords,
and oceans of frozen turquoise.

I could easily eat a peach.
Sprinklers wave softly in the dusk,
dousing the stranger newly arrived.
The drops, drying, change to steam.

Report on a Summer Evening

One red ball rolling
Two mauve-colored doves on a wire cooing
Three newspapers in blue plastic waiting at the end of a driveway
Four people in orange T-shirts hovering over a picnic table
Five mottled brown rabbits still as stones on the dry grass
Six yellow porch lights gleaming
Seven Styrofoam cups scattered on a baseball diamond
Eight children in multicolored shirts looking for one red ball
Nine grey cats turning into shadows
Ten magenta echinaceas glowing in the dusk
Eleven black bats flitting
Twelve trees shaking a mess of dark greenery
Who can guess how many cicadas singing?

Ode to Autumn Leaves

From behind our windows,
we watch the yard service
do in the leaves, bagging
heaps of outmoded finery
for disposal at curbside.

Once we owned the leaves.
Midwesterners with few
shorelines, we collected
leaves like shells.

Discriminating between
the gaudy and the subtle,
they were flashy talismans
in our ordinary childhoods.

We ironed their brightness
between wax paper,
trapped them in treasure boxes
until their color bled into air.

We flung leaves about us
as feather boas and capes
and gamboled among them
with squirrels and voles.

We raked them into
labyrinths and temples,
believing we could plot
the earth to our own design.

Tumbling into burial,
we quickly scattered our
garish cerements, giddy
masters of resurrection.

In those days, we finished
off the leaves by firing
them up in funeral pyres,
glorying to see them soar,
once more flamboyant.

Walking in Leaves

After spring and summer
of sticking to sidewalks,
I'm in the gutter
gallivanting among
the gaudy leaves.

I step on masses
of small, yellow
honey locust leaves.
I listen to them
sigh and collapse
underfoot, crumpled.

I'm on the lawn,
rushing headlong
through maple, oak,
sassafras, sycamore,
and redbud leaves,

splashing through
them like surf,
kicking them up into
bits of brittle spume.
I trample the earth

as I did as a child,
releasing the scent
of mold, gleefully
sadistic, leaving
trails of crushed leaves
in my wake.

Kansas Dusk: Early Fall

In an amber hiatus between day and dark,
we are spellbound, weightless.
In a cone of light, two couples play cards,
momentarily indifferent to winning or losing.
In his garage, a man pauses before an easel,
his brush a bone between his teeth.
A young woman stands on a curb. She carries
a pot of chrysanthemums before her
like a chalice. A man, gilded with sweat,
jogs toward her. From a position of command
on a front porch, a cat washes between her toes.
The sky's golden underbelly sags.
In an instant, before anyone decides
which card to play, it could suffocate us all.

Before the Freeze

Just before the freeze,
nothing is settled.
Everything's up in the air,
fluttering in transition.

Overhead, gulls unravel
in uncertain patterns.
Leaves swoop about in droves,
impossible for gravity to herd.

Wind sends the last
yellow sulfurs drifting
like scraps of memo paper
over the garden's dried stalks.

Imprisoned behind a storm
window, flies are wound up.
In a frenetic final scurry,
they pursue life, liberty, etc.

Some stress may be resolved
in hibernation or migration.
But like the flies, I imagine
I'll continue my own little flurry.

Winter Air

Winter's fierce air
crystallizes, becomes
ghostly breath, rims
nostrils, darts shards.

Winter's fierce air
swirls low over streets,
sweeps upward, gusts
of steaming whiteness
in Zen patterns.

Winter's fierce air
is invisible
in benign seasons.

Icicles

With the temperature indecisive,
between freezing and dripping,
gravity makes up its mind,
dribbling meticulously from
eaves and roofs into icicles.
One drop deliberately follows
another until the house is fringed.

It happens so sedately you hardly
notice, as in those friendships,
which, reduced to chilly words,
congeal inertly until you become
gelid and barred by fangs, clamped
within the whale's white ribs.

Truce

Just as I gave up on winter,
the snows came, soundlessly
falling through the night,
muffling streets, drifting
against houses, padding trees,
and I woke to a hush of light.

Out my window, each twig,
each limb was bandaged
in white. Burdened,
boughs bent to touch
the grasses, and the grasses
bent to touch the earth.

Scarred yards were mended.
Wrapped in the snow's
soft linen, trash disappeared.
Divisions between streets
and lawns dissolved
as everywhere snow smoothed
and soothed, spreading
a white flag across the land
and brokering with despair.

The Heart of Winter

As the snow slashes
in blue diagonals
across window panes,
you might see
the heart of winter as
a red cardinal singing
or a glowing wood stove
pulsating golden heat.

As the snow solemnly
fills dark ridges in fields,
you might experience
the heart of winter as
sluicing across sheer
sheets of white ice
or friends toasting
around a dinner table.

As streets turn slick
with invisible black ice,
you might feel
the heart of winter as
an eagle, shot dead,
its talons yanked out
or a man under blankets
on a sidewalk heating vent.

As the cold chills my blood,
the heart of winter is
my South African mother
lost and looking for me
in the snow.

Winter Exposure

In winter, the shape
of things comes clear.
Stripped of their leafy
finery, trees show their
branched skeletons.
Their intricate tracery
is up against the pale
sky for inspection.

The maple twigs' finger
bones, the oak limbs'
sturdier knuckles and
vertebrae, reveal a trajectory
of upward yearning.
The locust bares its claws.

The nests of birds and
squirrels, obscured by
summer green, are exposed
like organs in a chart,
secret sites of vitality
in another season.

Freezing a creek's
glib fluidity, ice stills
its surface into a lens.
I may prefer spring thaw,
but only ice discloses
a creek's snarled roots
and pebbled depths.

Melt-Down

Eternal snow, galaxies
disintegrating, celestial
ceilings flaking, it's life
inside an Atomic Bomb Ring
from a long-ago Wheaties box.

Apocalyptic climate change
redesigns suburbs: rectangles
are eliminated, chairs left
out overnight and cars
are molded into mounds.
Drifts slouch against garages.
A few telephone poles
determine the perpendicular.
Sidewalks and driveways
no longer divide lawns.
Blank fields stretch to a faded
horizon. Nothing sparkles.

Cartons of recyclables topple,
and the garbage stays inside.
Makeup holds no interest.
Calendars and taste lose
all meaning. I hibernate all day
in rank, long underwear.
Others bicker, drink all night,
neglect the baby, and claim
the other one did it. Grandmothers
are a nuisance. Suicide answers
to imperfection, and if jailed,
bail is set beyond all means.

Finally, the long-awaited thaw,
days of mist, soft and treacherous.
Angles are restored but pose
no resistance as substances
evaporate into damp particles.

Icicles lengthen, sharpen,
shatter like ceramic figurines
on front stoops. I stride out
into oceanic moisture, dependent
on headlights to direct me.
Exhaust soot and sludge edge
the remnants. Ice ridges mark
thoroughfares. Streetlights,
surrounded in gauze, waver
in the haze, each a planet with
its system of swirling microbes.
Spring remains a cliché.

Domestic Sublime

Both lake and sky
stretched out
like clean linen,
ironed, pressed,
starched, unworn,
except for marks
above by geese,
stitching invisible
seams, and below
by the lace tracery
of rodent tracks.

Coming along
the horizon, the boom,
a white echo, might
be sonic, volcanic,
or only glacial plates
rearranging the lake's
simple garments.

Summer in Winter

In the cocoon of winter
you think of bulbs, snug
under earth and snow's
layers of flannel,
and of yourself, younger,
naked in summer heat,
baking bread at midnight,
your breasts aglow like
loaves, plump, full, rising
in the moonlight.

3.
Unusual Weather

Independence Day

A fireworks ban in effect,
the neighborhood rested
from war. No traffic stirred.
Children came outside again.
Hydrangeas turned lavender.
Cats lounged. Cicadas whined.
I heard the earthworms churn.
Something disturbed the air:
a catfish, glittering blue, walked
up from the river, called in
a swirl of flies, a raucous buzz,
and sprawled, exhausted,
slime-silvered, in the yard.

Wash Day

All day, the storm's washing
machine churns clouds like
Olympian sheets and towels,
tossing them about the sky.
Their suds swirl, and thunderous
flapping signals malfunction.
The strained air tightens.
Any minute, the latch will snap
in a gush of wind and water.

We take the cats to the basement
and sit among the crickets.
The gale flagellates the house.
Overhead, it slashes the roof.
Underground, we hear rivers
sluicing through sewers. Will
it take forty days to gyrate through
these cycles of rinse and spin?

The Aftermath

Helter-skelter, branches
lie cast around the yard
in a design no I-Ching
soothsayer could decipher.
Telephone wires twist
runically across the grass.
Random shingles provide
diacritical markings.
A clear and windless sky
spells out the only clue.

Signs and Portents in the Heartland

The heavens fill with signs
and portents. Around suppertime
on 9/11, the Kansas sky
was clear of contrails. Only
a sundog, a slice of rainbow,
gleamed above the western
horizon like a small billboard.

Celestial navigation shows
Venus in transit. The azimuth
of Mars shimmies toward
the sun. In winter, rainbows
arrive like migrating parrots.
Plumed spectra linger at the edge
of clouds. Cumulonimbus clouds
are mango-tinged, palpable,
and close enough to eat, and
the contrails have once more
zippered the sky open.

Rainbow Sign

Through the kitchen window,
I watched the gold-flecked shower
signaling a rainbow's imminence.

Its arrival was soundless, radiant,
a surprise quivering in the air,
an iridescent arc emerging from mist.

In the bright drizzle, I felt foxes
dressed in ancient courtly garments,
gathering for a wedding.

Neighbors stood in the shining street,
mesmerized by such trembling,
by half a halo over ordinary roofs.

Once Noah heeded the rainbow sign.
Once I walked a rainbow bridge spanning
Andean peaks. Momentary portents,

rainbows linger long enough to mark
memories. Once a double rainbow over
Maui was repeated in a humpback's spout,

glistening over and over, again and again.
Like some poems, lost, rediscovered,
rainbows chime on.

New Year's Eve, 1998

Not since 1915 has a full moon
appeared on New Year's Eve.

Through the day, they posted
warnings: "Blizzard conditions.
Travelers' advisory." The air
remained alert, and a sundog
flashed the spectrum through
ice crystals. Later the moon,
a wobbling orb, unsteady
in its curious visit, backlit
the night from behind
curdling clouds. We proceeded
with our usual ceremonies:
charades, champagne, whistles.

In the countryside, at midnight,
the coyotes devoured
the last rabbit, and in the city,
a gangly hound, tail up like a stalk,
galloped down the center line
of the main highway, hell-bent
for somewhere.

Plagues

That spring, heading for the woods,
I anticipated light to be rafting
through the trees, newly leafed.
I hadn't expected a canopy so tattered,
or the sun piercing so many holes.

And then I saw the hackberry trunks,
dark pillars wriggling with caterpillars
whose frass fell on my face, rain-soft.
And then I heard the warblers and orioles
crunching caterpillars in between trills.

Though the frogs are not yet in my bed
or my oven, Egypt's plagues—water
bleeding from fracking, horses dying
of pigeon fever, mosquitoes from
West Nile, a barrage of wild hurricanes
and tornadoes—are upon us.

That night the hackberry caterpillars,
morphed into gaudy, many-eyed butterflies,
swirled out of a bottled childhood dream
to smother me.

Drought in November

Inside the glass globe,
red petals circle the burning
bush in a ring of fire.
The leaves of maples and
sycamores lie rumpled
in the gutters, and only
the oaks cling to their leaves.
Shaken, they will all be
roused, and snow will swirl.

But every day, the sun
sears through the glass,
and no snow falls in Moscow.
The winter wheat pales
on the stalk, and the river
sinks further into sludge.
Barges are stymied,
and slowly the ancient
messages on river rocks,
millennia under water,
are revealed, illegible.

4.

The Death of Bivalves

The Death of Bivalves

Sewer-diggers excavate
the hard clay in my yard.
Clod after clod, they throw
the solidified sea up onto
itself, reaching for a broken
pipe in the murky depths.

They shovel through
cemeteries of corals and
crinoids, indifferent to
the myriad deaths of bivalves
composted in this earth,
the same as the bones
of the boy on a motorcycle,
tossed over a Jeep's hood
at the neighborhood corner,
where plastic flowers freshen
his memorial.

Amber

Stones tell the great beasts'
genealogies, their teeth and bones
laid out across landscapes
like ceremonial necklaces,
but smaller beings are preserved
in pools of stagnant sunlight.
Transparent, three-dimensional,
they reveal their inner lives,
their blood and guts, hold out
their wings, hold high their pinchers
with exquisite articulation,
opaque, concentrated poems.

The Return of the Animals

The polar bear pivots on a chunk of ice.
The Siberian tiger pauses and prowls on.
Others won't stay down or in their niches.
They keep disappearing, reappearing,
not only in dreams and Disney remakes.
With a stranger's indifference, an ornate
box turtle saunters through my backyard.

Blithely, I throw a bouquet of roses into
the garbage can, and they spread out across
a heap of dingy grey fur—a raccoon corpse,
a pile of rats, a snoozing feral cat—until
the possum, resurrected from playing dead,
stares me down, spreading his wide, pink
bubblegum smile, set with milky teeth.
His people were here long before mine.

Take Nothing for Granted

In the distance, tilting,
a young golden eagle;
in the winter garden,
a rufous hummingbird.

Grackles gorging,
screeching, terrifying
chickadees and finches,
then rising up, swaying,
twisting, spreading
into a flowing murmuration.

Condor chicks, fed
by puppets, wearing
radios and IDs, return
to Bitter Creek. Avoiding
power lines and people,
they resume their soaring.

Reduced to eighteen,
whooping cranes
spread their wings
in a last Ghost Dance,
when one of them
learned to love a man,
to dance with him,
to build a nest with him,
to lay twin eggs so that
whoopers continue
prancing and dancing.

Snowy owls,
ghostly and steadfast,
saving Hogwarts from
Voldemort, camouflaged
head to feathery toe
for Arctic survival,

starving in the world's
whiteness, flying south
for mice and moles,
die in prairie ditches.

Dreams of Flight

For Marion Foster

Last night, hummingbirds
darted into her dreams'
thick greenery, glittering
and quick as stars loosened
from night to spin shining
invisible threads around
flowers, leaves, insects.

Tonight, the eagles come
swooping in platoons over
her bright river of dreams,
their wings banners unfurling,
their feathers rippling
with sunrise colors, with one
among them, albino, spangled
and shaping the air.

Overhead, through night's
layered shelves, lapland
longspurs fly, crying *pew, pew,*
whistling in the dark. Seeking
earth, they crash into city lights.
Their bodies, limp brown bags
discovered at day break,
litter lampposts.

The Dead Sparrow

The sparrow slammed against my house.
It was not an easy death. Fouled in excrement,
it lay in a porch corner, a wadded handkerchief,
a throwaway bird.

It fit into my hand's cup, a lightweight,
hollow bones and fluff of feathers perfected
to do what I cannot: rise above fear.
Feet curled under, always it was prepared to soar.

Walking woods and prairies, I find no bird bones.
Only this one sparrow came to me in death,
amulet to cherish for invisible skeletons
consecrating the earth everywhere.

Invasive Species

The pintails are lifting
clamorously from the canals,
wings whirring whirligigs
of anxiety. Behind them,
water spreads in agitated circles.
Sparrows rise up in a twitter.
Deer flash me their white tails,
the high sign of rejection.
How did I give myself away?
My jacket's whispering nylon?
My breath, scent, heavy shadow?

Walking into the wetlands,
careful not to rustle reeds,
sidestepping noisy seeping,
I thought I'd trod possum-soft.
Delicately, I unlatched greenbrier
bushes and wild roses, boughs
flung across my path, and
avoided the crunch of twigs.
Committed voyeur of the wild,
I cannot slither, but I have learned
to creep.

I keep forgetting that my kind
is prone to pandemonium.
Crossing more boundaries
than zebra mussel or mongoose,
we resonate upon the earth.

Facing Catastrophe

Geology records the Great Dying,
insects and dinosaurs pressed
together, roaring and whimpering,
as the meteorite exploded.
Swamps smoldered, and a nimbus
of stench shrouded the planet for eons.

Noah, gathering his herds and flocks
together, felt a tremor through
his sandals in the quivering air.
Floating dry in the ark, he witnessed
his neighbors swimming aimlessly.
When he could land again,
his fields were planted with corpses.

Krakatoa, spewing fire out of water,
incinerated islands and sent rafts of
ash and pumice to scour the shores
of distant continents. A scrim filtered
the sun, and with skies blazing, a man
on an icy bridge in Norway held up
his hands and screams forever.

Alongside catastrophe, a twig
swivels steadily in a creek's current,
worrying the water, hollowing
out a sandy sinkhole. So do wasps
patiently paste their grey globes
together, and peonies unfold a petal
at a time.

Soundings

Through the seas, a cacophony
of conversation clatters, clicks,
and crackles, connecting krill
with krill, urchin with urchin.
On the surface, porpoises slap
out melodious sighs and signals,
while deep down, humpback whales
sing this year's latest hits
and the sperm whales' ears,
their convolutions of densest ivory,
see sounds beyond mountains.
The white coral seethes.

Through the earth, loam-thickened
drum skin, a resonance of riffs,
cats padding, coyotes scampering,
a whisk and slither of lizards,
the heartbeats of moles pattering.
In caves, the echoes of stones, honed
and rounded by millennia, hum and thrum.
Elephants, standing stolidly, grasping
the ground, hear through their toenails
the thumps of continental change:
the stamp of jackhammers, oil rigs.
The white roots of trees, exposed, scream.

Through the air, a transmission of bulletins:
hoots, howls, wails, warbles, babbles, buzzes,
screeches, squeaks, rhapsodies, blasphemies.
Who doesn't have something to say?
Frogs and folks collaborate in choruses,
and crows conduct congressional hearings.
Unseen gust, bluster, breeze identify themselves
in roaring roof, creaking branch, whispering grass.
White clouds, mutating to ultraviolet, swell.

Watching Trains

Out driving,
you can still encounter trains
rolling through the country,
one car following another,
rolling smoothly, ceaselessly,
carrying coal, automobiles,
stacked containers coast-to-coast,
crisscrossing the country,
barging through the country,
snaking through the country,
trains moving on endlessly,
moving bulldozers, trailers,
passing crossings blinking,
barriers clanging down,
everything stopped,
while trains charge through,
past cars waiting,
carrying the steady sound
of oiled rumbling, churning
into the silence of the country.
Watching trains, you will see
wheels turning, shafts grinding,
and you will not see a single soul.

Mammals Asleep

Billowed by waves, whale snoozes,
drifting among the flotsam of dreams.

Elephants doze, bolstering one another,
leaning deliberately and delicately.

Fox digs down into sleep's den, cushions
herself with darkness and a fiery tail.

Mice, in a slumbering mound, still run
mazes through grasses, never losing their way.

Cat and I, synchronizing snores, stretch
out our limbs and learn to fly.

Mending Meadows

Celebrate meadows
where fertilizer is free,
decaying dandelions
and mildewing acorns;
where a tree lays its shadow
down gently onto grass;
where mushrooms assume
startling and lavish shapes;
where weeds are flowers—
white clover, yellow oxalis,
wild violets, lilies of the valley—
and spread roots through moss;
where rabbits and turtles roam;
where during the night
spiders spin it together
into a shimmering whole,
and in the early morning
wet grasses reflect a full
spectrum of colors, which
is how fields once were,
how lawns might be.

The Day After Christmas

It was global warming's gift.
White Christmas melted overnight,
snow's ragged edges on the curbs.
At noon, I walked out into spring.
From my neighbor's porch,
wind chimes tinkled, remnants of
ice crackling. Red bows fluttered
aimlessly in the wind. Farther down
the street, flashing pink ribbons
girded the trunks of a redbud
and three hackberries, doomed
for growing into telephone lines.
Evergreen boughs, fading along
a fence, drooped with melting snow
and a burden of Christmas bunting.
On a bungalow's south side,
plastic perennials sprang, multi-
colored, from the moist earth's bed.

The Measure of Light

What is the yardstick
for light-years? Where
is the scale? I cannot
weigh those summer days,
so clear, the opposite shore
came floating toward me.
I cannot measure this
winter light lengthening
toward spring, stretching
to course with sap, sinking
into the recalcitrant hearts
of rhizomes and bulbs.

Linked

For David Abram

1. *July, Early Morning: Higgins Lake, Michigan*

We were three in a boat, one dog,
out by the island when the fog
scrolled in, a density of white,
erasing us, our shores. We drifted,
muffled in plush silence, listening
for buoys, hearing only a loon's
cosmic laughter.

2. *September, High Noon: Wakarusa Wetlands, Kansas*

Within this dome of heat,
grasshoppers rouse and whirr.
Breathlessly the monarchs
coast, hover, settle on asters,
sunflowers, thistles, giving
wings to petals and lifting
me with them into the air.

3. *February, Twilight: Wakarusa Wetlands, Kansas*

Heaped with molten light, clouds
become luminous tissues, streamers
trembling on the surfaces of pond
and canal. Overhead, the birds rise
into the light's farthest reaches, layers
over layers, designs spreading.

4. *April, Night: Bali, Indonesia*

He awakened in the hillside hut
to quivering darkness and felt
his way to the door. From the threshold,
he stepped into living light. Overhead,
strange constellations. Far below,
lanterns, villagers, singing, dancing.
In between, multiple terraces, mirrors
in which pulsating fireflies reflected
the stars everywhere.

Mene, Mene, Tekel, Upharsin

The writing hand taps oaks
and asters on the motherboard,
signaling the sky where cumulus
clouds puff out the message,
soon erased by winds, while
the tapping continues, touching
lightly on polar bears and coral,
sending long striations parallel
to the horizon in prismatic colors,
the writing hand moving along,
shifting and deleting, tap tap,
capitalizing here and there,
mammoths and mosasaurs among
the curling cirrus, clicking home
where icons sprawl like microbes
across a sea of soundless waves.

Acknowledgments

Begin Again: 150 Kansas Poems, ed. Caryn Mirriam-Goldberg, for "How to Read a Winter Field"

Friends of the Kansas River website for "Watching the Kansas River"

Interdisciplinary Studies in Literature and the Environment for "Heat Sequence: In and Out of Dreams"

The Midwest Quarterly for "Domestic Sublime"

Sprout for "The Calm Place"

Types and Shadows for "Prairie Immersion: After 9/11," previously titled "Konza Prairie"

The Wakarusa Wetlands in Word and Image for "Spring Jazz" and parts four, five, and six from "November Meditations," previously titled "Tracks," "A Yearning for Beavers," and "The Little Birds"

Cover painting, "Green Hills," by Lisa Grossman; cover and interior book design by Diane Kistner (dkistner@futurecycle.org); Gentium Book Basic text and titling

About FutureCycle Press

FutureCycle Press is dedicated to publishing lasting English-language poetry books, chapbooks, and anthologies in both print-on-demand and ebook formats. Founded in 2007 by long-time independent editor/publishers and partners Diane Kistner and Robert S. King, the press incorporated as a nonprofit in 2012. A number of our editors are distinguished poets and writers in their own right, and we have been actively involved in the small press movement going back to the early seventies.

The FutureCycle Poetry Book Prize and honorarium is awarded annually for the best full-length volume of poetry we publish in a calendar year. Introduced in 2013, our Good Works projects are devoted to issues of universal significance, with all proceeds donated to a related worthy cause. Our Selected Poems series highlights contemporary poets with a substantial body of work to their credit.

We are dedicated to giving all of the authors we publish the care their work deserves, making our catalog of titles the most diverse and distinguished it can be, and paying forward any earnings to fund more great books.

We've learned a few things about independent publishing over the years. We've also evolved a unique, resilient publishing model that allows us to focus mainly on vetting and preserving for posterity the most books of exceptional quality without becoming overwhelmed with bookkeeping and mailing, fundraising activities, or taxing editorial and production "bubbles." To find out more about what we are doing, come see us at www.futurecycle.org.